Written by Starlyn J. First
Designed by Sandra Bruner

an imprint of
SCHOLASTIC
www.scholastic.com

Published by Tangerine Press, an imprint of Scholastic Inc., 557 Broadway; New York, NY 10012

10 9 8 7 6 5 4 3 2 1
ISBN-10: 0-545-10691-5
ISBN-13: 978-0-545-10691-7

Printed and manufactured in China

Contents

Prank Time!

Pulling stunts and practical jokes (or pranks) on your friends and family is so much fun. Just wait until you experience all the hilarity once they realize what's up! You know the feeling you get when someone makes you laugh? It makes you feel pretty great, right? Now, you'll have the opportunity to make others laugh, and that feels just as great!

So, carefully choose the people on whom you want to play a practical joke. We'll call them your "victims." It just means the joke's on them! Also, choose the stunt to match the victim carefully. The best people to pull pranks on usually are members of your immediate family at a big family reunion, or your friends at a party. So, have fun and share a lot of laughs!

Excuse You!

THE STUNT: Making other people in the room think that someone cut the cheese. (And we don't mean the cheddar with a knife—wink-wink!)

THE TARGET: Pick out someone who usually has good manners or who embarrasses easily. A red-faced blusher is the best!

STUFF YOU'LL NEED: The whoopee cushion in your kit.

SKILLS YOU SHOULD/CAN USE: You need to be observant to choose the right victim. Also, you need to be quick—quick with your thoughts and quick with your hands.

ACTION! You've found your victim. Now, when it looks like she is about to sit down, quickly go behind her and lay the whoopee cushion on the seat. You have to be quick! (Note: If you don't care who your victim is, just leave the whoopee cushion under the couch or chair cushion and let the noise begin!)

HINT-HINT: Wait until there are a lot of people around, but in a room that's not too noisy. (Gotta hear the cheese being cut!) A good time might be when you're at a family party and the gang is ready to sit down to eat.

REALLY HELPFUL HINT: Don't let the people in the room see you walking around with the whoopee cushion. (That would ruin the surprise, right?) Keep it hidden until you're ready to move.

SEE WHAT HAPPENS!

Once your victim sits down and the "fart" erupts, everyone in the room will become silent and look at your victim. Oh, no! They'll be shocked that your victim could be so rude, and not even try to hide it! Watch as your victim's face turns beet red!

Sour Taste in the Mouth

THE STUNT: To leave a bad taste in someone's mouth—one he was not expecting.

THE TARGET: Anyone with a toothbrush.

STUFF YOU'LL NEED: Go to the kitchen and get something sour, like lemon, lime, or pickle juice. You can choose other tastes, too, like something bitter or tangy. But be careful! Don't use anything dangerous or really hot.

ACTION! Make sure no one's around and grab your victim's toothbrush. Soak it in the chosen juice for a minute. Shake off the liquid (but don't rinse it), and put the toothbrush back where you found it.

SEE WHAT HAPPENS! Your victim will begin to brush his teeth as usual. All of a sudden, he will experience the strange taste, yell "Eww!", and grab for a cup to rinse with water. Gag!

Mom! I Have Lice!

THE STUNT: Making your parents believe you have a really bad case of lice or dandruff. (Grownups hate that stuff!)

THE TARGET: Your parents or guardians.

STUFF YOU'LL NEED: Find some coarse salt, like sea salt. That's the kind of salt that comes in big crystals. You also can use very fine, dried breadcrumbs.

ACTION! Sprinkle the salt or breadcrumbs on top of your head. Do it in front of a mirror so you are careful not to use too much. It has to look realistic! Go find your parents and start a casual conversation. Act like nothing is different and wait for them to notice your "dandruff." (Try not to smile or laugh. You don't want to give anything away!)

SEE WHAT HAPPENS! Watch the horror come over their faces as they notice "lice" or "dandruff" on your head. Disgusting! Prepare to be hauled into the bathroom or the yard so they can try to do something about it!

You're Late for Work!

THE STUNT: Making your parents or an older sibling believe they overslept for work or school.

THE TARGET: The best family member to pick is the one who is a deep sleeper—the one who really needs an alarm clock to get up in the morning.

STUFF YOU'LL NEED: Your victim's alarm clock.

SKILLS YOU CAN USE: You have to be able to stay awake longer than your victim, or get yourself up earlier. (You'll probably need an alarm clock, too!)

ACTION! While your victim is sleeping, quietly go into her room and set the clock one hour ahead. Then turn off the set alarm. When you get up (early!), get dressed as you normally would, depending on what day it is, and go into your victim's room at "8 A.M." (Remember, it's really 7 A.M.!). Start to wake your victim up by saying, "Hey, do you know what time it is?!" or "Why are you still in bed?!"

HINT-HINT: Make sure your alarm clock is set correctly, so you can get up at the right time to make this work. Also, you might want to figure out how to work your victim's alarm clock before you try this stunt. And if you make breakfast or coffee for her, she'll actually have extra time to enjoy it—and she might not be so mad!

SEE WHAT HAPPENS! Your parents or siblings will shoot up off their pillow, eyes wide, look over at their clock, and jump out of bed. Watch as they run around frantically, trying to get ready for work or school. Hilarious!

Eek! There's a Bug in My Drink!

THE STUNT: Making people believe there are insects in their drinks. Eww, contamination!

THE TARGET: Anyone you see with a drink in his hand.

STUFF YOU'LL NEED: The fake flies in your kit.

SKILLS YOU SHOULD/CAN USE: Quick hands!

ACTION! When you're pretty sure no one is looking, drop some of the fake flies in someone's drink, a filled pitcher, or a punch bowl.

HINT-HINT: If it takes a long time for someone to notice the fake flies, just point to the drink or punch bowl and say, "Eww, gross! There's a bug in there!"

SEE WHAT HAPPENS! The ones who were enjoying their drinks will feel ill from the thought that they just drank an insect's bathwater. Let the gagging and spitting begin!

Another way to pull off this prank is to freeze the flies in ice cubes. Fill an ice cube tray with water, and then drop in the flies. Put the tray in the freezer, and after a couple of hours, your fly-filled ice cubes are ready for major gross-out action!

There's Fruit Punch on the Rug!

THE STUNT: Freaking people out by making them believe there's spilled fruit punch on an important item. There are lots of places to pull this prank, such as the computer keyboard, your mom's favorite dress, or a sibling's school project.

WARNING: Food coloring will stain! Make sure to lay newspaper down over your work area and clean up as soon as you're done.

THE TARGET: Anyone, anywhere.

STUFF YOU'LL NEED: This one will take a little planning on your part, but it's worth it! You'll need a disposable cup, disposable spoon, disposable bowl, white school glue, and red food coloring.

You'll need three or four days of prep time to prepare the prop for this prank.

ACTION! Check out the recipe for the spilled fruit punch on the next page. Just follow the directions, and when the fake stuff is ready, put it wherever you decide is best for the most fun (well, for you, anyway!).

GLUE

HINT-HINT:

This is very important! DO NOT place the fake fruit punch on a warm surface (like the computer's monitor, tower, or hard-drives)! Since you're using glue, your creation might soften on a warm surface and ruin it.

SEE WHAT HAPPENS!

This is a good one. Your victim's day will drastically change when she sees this mess on her stuff! Watch as she runs around trying to find a way to clean it up. And who would do such a thing?!

Spilled Fruit Punch Recipe

1. **Using a disposable spoon, measure out three spoonfuls of glue into a disposable bowl.**
2. **Add two or three drops of red food coloring to the glue. Keep adding the food coloring, one drop at a time, until the glue is the color you want. Stir the mixture with the disposable spoon.**
3. **Pour a little bit of the glue mixture into a disposable cup. Then, lay the cup on its side on a piece of wax paper. Pour the rest of the glue mixture onto the wax paper in front of the cup.**
4. **Hide the whole thing and let it set for three or four days. If it's cold outside, it might take a little longer.**
5. **After the third or fourth day, try touching the "fruit punch." If it feels dry on your finger, carefully and slowly peel off the wax paper. It's now okay to put the fruit punch on the surface you've chosen!**

Short-sheeting

THE STUNT: You can annoy and frustrate someone who is tired and ready for bed (because he won't be getting to sleep right away!).

THE TARGET: Anyone in the house who usually makes his bed. If it's someone who doesn't, the made-up bed will look too suspicious.

STUFF YOU'LL NEED: A bed with a matching set of sheets and a comforter or bedspread.

SKILLS YOU SHOULD/CAN USE: How to make a bed! If you don't know how, practice before you do this stunt.

ACTION! Choose your victim and go into his bedroom when you know he'll be gone for a while. Then, follow these steps to rig his bed!

1. **Leave the bottom sheet alone (the one that's fitted to the mattress). Take the top sheet and spread it over the bottom one.**
2. **Fold over the bottom half to the top so the sheet is folded in half.**
3. **Tuck the top sheet into the bottom of the mattress. Fold down the top area of the sheet, just like your victim normally does.**
4. **Put the pillows and comforter or bedspread where they belong.**

SEE WHAT HAPPENS! Your tired victim will get into bed, and then find he can't stretch out his legs! Why? Because you've "short-sheeted" his bed! He gets tangled up, confused, frustrated, and, well, probably not too happy, since he's so tired!

Your Sister's Shoe and Other Places to Put Bugs

THE STUNT: To freak someone out with bugs.

THE TARGET: Anyone who would be grossed out by bugs.

STUFF YOU'LL NEED: The fake flies in your kit.

ACTION! Put the fake flies in your victim's shoe, bed, bathtub, or cereal bowl (before she puts any food in it). You can always wedge a fly or two into something your victim uses every day–put one on a bar of soap or sticking out of her toothbrush bristles. Just make sure the flies are noticeable enough that she won't accidentally put them in her mouth!

HINT-HINT: One of the best places is inside a shoe. Stepping on something that shouldn't be in there really adds to the screams!

SEE WHAT HAPPENS! The funniest thing to happen will be the screams. Your victim might jump back and maybe even run from the "bugs." Then again, she might stomp hard on them, and then you'll be left with squashed props. Oh, well, it's still funny either way!

Gross! Is That What I Think It Is?

THE STUNT: Simply to gross out people!

WARNING: Food coloring will stain! Make sure to lay newspaper down over your work area, and clean up as soon as you're done.

THE TARGET: Anyone you want to gross out.

STUFF YOU'LL NEED: Instant oatmeal; dried peas, lentils, or dried soup mix (the more colorful, the better); tacky glue; and food coloring; disposable spoon and wax paper.

ACTION! Follow the recipe for fake vomit on the next page. Once you're finished, place the vomit anywhere in your house, somewhere public where people sit, or on a sidewalk where there are a lot of people.

SEE WHAT HAPPENS!
Watch from afar how people react to your disgusting "vomit"! Some will make a face, some can't get away fast enough, and some will do all they can to avoid stepping in it. If you put it on your living room carpet, watch your mom really freak out!

You'll need three or four days of prep time to prepare the prop for this prank.

WARNING:
DO NOT put the fake vomit on a warm surface (like a computer monitor, tower, or hard-drives)! The glue will soften and ruin it.

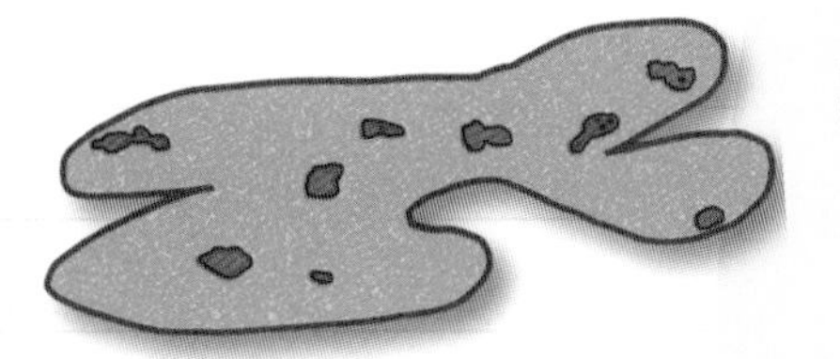

Recipe for Vomit

1. Using a disposable spoon, measure out four spoonfuls of glue, one spoonful of uncooked instant oatmeal, and a few drops each of red and yellow food coloring into a disposable bowl. Add as many drops of the food coloring as you need, one drop of each color at a time, to get an orange color. Mix well.
2. Pour the mixture onto wax paper.
3. Take the dried peas, lentils, or dried soup mix and sprinkle over the mixture. Gently press them down into the mixture so they're not just sitting on top.
4. Allow the mixture to dry for three or four days. If it's chilly outside, it might take longer.
5. When you touch it and it feels dry, slowly peel off the wax paper. Your vomit is ready!

This Computer's Driving Me Nuts!

THE STUNT: Making your parents or older siblings think there's something very wrong with the computer.

THE TARGET: Anyone using the computer.

STUFF YOU'LL NEED: A computer, mouse, and a sticky note.

ACTION! Cut a sticky note to fit the underside of the mouse, and write "Gotcha!" on it. Stick the note to the ball on the bottom of the mouse. Make sure it's cut small enough so that the paper doesn't show when the mouse is being used. When your victims try using the mouse, nothing will happen. No cursor, no clicking!

SEE WHAT HAPPENS! Your victims will get more and more frustrated as they mess around with the keyboard, monitor, and tower before they think to turn over the mouse. Then they'll see your "Gotcha!"

Refreshing Gum

THE STUNT: Offering someone gum, and then squirting him with water.

THE TARGET: Anyone who might want a piece of gum.

STUFF YOU'LL NEED: The fake squirt gum pack in your kit.

ACTION! Fill the plastic container with water and put it back into the fake gum pack. Replace the fake piece of gum. Then, offer a friend or family member some gum. When he says yes, hold out the pack of fake gum and squeeze it a little. Out squirts water!

HINT-HINT: You might want to keep some real gum around as a peace offering.

SEE WHAT HAPPENS! The person who started to take the "gum" and got squirted might start cracking up. Why? Because it's an old trick, and he won't believe he fell for it!

Hey, Dude! Pedicure?

THE STUNT: At camp or an overnighter, making a buddy spend the rest of the time there with painted toenails.

THE TARGET: It has to be a guy, and someone who will be wearing flip-flops or sandals, or who's involved in water activities where he's barefoot. It won't work in the winter when he's wearing socks and shoes.

STUFF YOU'LL NEED: A bottle of bright red or pink nail polish and a flashlight.

SKILLS YOU SHOULD/CAN USE: You should learn beforehand how to polish nails. If you're sloppy, a bad pedicure could add to the fun, but a perfect pedicure would be hilarious.

ACTION! Make sure your buddy is sound asleep. Sneak up quietly, turn the flashlight on his toes, and start painting. Do it quickly, but try to do a good job.

HINT-HINT: Try not to put the sheets back on his feet right after you've finished. The wet polish might stick to the sheet and ruin both the sheet and the polish job! Most importantly, make sure there's no nail polish remover anywhere around!

SEE WHAT HAPPENS! Unless he's very observant, your buddy will be the last one to realize his toenails are painted that bright color. How will he finally know? Everyone will be pointing at them, laughing out loud!

Stop That Ringing!

THE STUNT: Annoying someone with ringing alarm clocks everywhere.

THE TARGET: Anyone who really dislikes waking up in the morning.

STUFF YOU'LL NEED: As many alarm clocks as you can find. Borrow them from friends if you need to. They have to be battery-powered since you'll be hiding them all over.

SKILLS YOU SHOULD/CAN USE: The ability to set alarm clocks, and good hiding skills.

ACTION! You can set the alarm clocks beforehand in your room, and have them ready so you can sneak them into your victim's room when she's not around. Set them to go off at an early-morning hour. But set each one three minutes later than the last one. If you're using a few clock radios, make sure they're set to a really loud, hard rock music station. If you can find some clocks with loud buzzers, your prank will be even more annoying! Hide the clocks all over your victim's bedroom, like in the closet, on a shelf, under the bed, in a dresser drawer, and on a windowsill behind the curtains.

HINT-HINT: Make sure you pull this stunt on a weekend, or a day when your victim usually sleeps in—or tries to! Also, she probably won't be a happy camper after this stunt, so have breakfast ready to help with the forgiveness factor.

SEE WHAT HAPPENS! Watch or listen from outside your victim's door. She'll be going nuts trying to find all the alarm clocks going off every three minutes. She might come running out of the room in panic mode because she can't take it anymore!

Quick! It's Quicksand!

THE STUNT: Astound everyone around you as you turn liquid into solid, and then back again to liquid.

THE TARGET: Anyone who wants to be astounded (and get a little messy!).

STUFF YOU'LL NEED: Cornstarch and water.

SKILLS YOU SHOULD/CAN USE: Fast hands and great cleanup skills.

ACTION! To make the "quicksand," mix 1 cup (236.5 ml) of cornstarch with ¼ cup (59 ml) of water. Add a little water at a time until you get something that looks like pancake mix. Use your hands to mix it together quickly. The faster you go, the more solid the mixture gets. Turn it into any shape you want just by squeezing and molding it. But what's this? As soon as you stop touching it and mixing it with your hands, it turns back into a liquid goop!

This prank is very messy. If you can, prepare for it near the sink, and make sure to have lots of paper towels handy!

SEE WHAT HAPPENS! Now, hand the solid mix (keep it moving!) to a friend or family member. Oops, too bad—did you forget to tell him it'll turn back to liquid if it's not played with? Ha-ha, the joke's on him! (Real quicksand works the same way. Touching it makes it solid; leaving it alone turns it back to liquid.)

Cleanup on Aisle Three...

WARNING:

DO NOT dump the mixture down the drain when you're finished, because the drain might get clogged. Place the mixture in a plastic bag and throw it in the garbage can.

Just Another Cereal Gag

THE STUNT: To make someone pour out all the contents of a box of cereal.

If the box of cereal is pretty full, pour some of the contents into a clean container to put back in the box later. You don't want to get in trouble for ruining an entire box of perfectly edible cereal!

THE TARGET: Anyone who's hungry.

STUFF YOU'LL NEED: A box of o-shaped cereal and a long piece of string.

ACTION! Pour out the contents of the box. String together all of the cereal, and then tie the ends of the string together. Carefully put the cereal back in the box.

SEE WHAT HAPPENS! Your hungry victim will eagerly try to pour out the cereal, and when it finally comes out of the box, she'll be shocked and confused to see that it's all tied together. (As a peace offering, you might want to offer her some of the untouched cereal that you put aside earlier!)

What, Did That Tickle?

THE STUNT: Making someone rub shaving or whipped cream all over her face, but without her knowing it.

THE TARGET: Anyone who is a sound sleeper and also has a really good sense of humor.

STUFF YOU'LL NEED: Shaving cream or whipped cream and a feather (or something else light that will tickle a nose).

ACTION! Quietly walk over to your soundly sleeping victim. Put shaving or whipped cream on both of her hands (palms) as quietly as you can. Then, tickle her nose with the feather. She'll eventually reach up to try to scratch the itch. Keep doing this until both hands have made a big mess on her face.

HINT-HINT: As a peace offering, have a towel or washcloth ready.

SEE WHAT HAPPENS! Your victim will be so bothered by the tickling or itch that she won't know what's happening until it's too late. Plus, if she's a really sound sleeper, it might take a while for her to wake up and figure it out! Messy, messy!

Look What I Found!

THE STUNT: Making someone believe you found a box with a cut-off finger in it!

THE TARGET: Anyone who gets really grossed out by blood and body parts.

STUFF YOU'LL NEED: Small box with a lid, cotton balls, and ketchup or fake blood. You can find fake blood at party supply stores or gag shops, especially during Halloween time.

ACTION! Follow these steps to gross someone out!

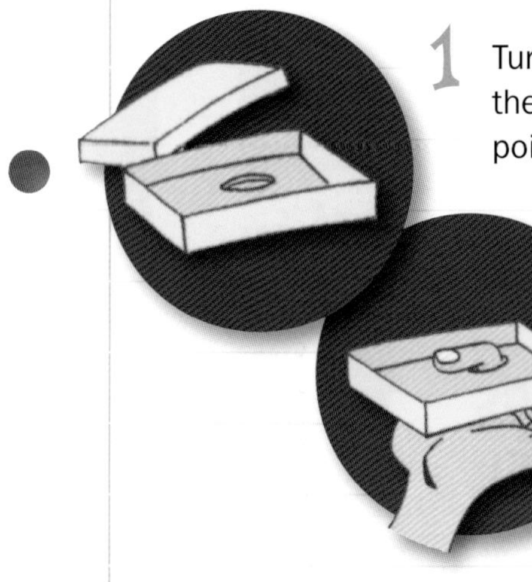

1 Turn the box over and cut a hole on the bottom big enough to put your pointer finger through.

2 Once your finger is fit in the box, put enough cotton balls around it so it looks like the finger is lying on top of them.

3 Then, squirt a small amount of ketchup or fake blood around the knuckle (not too much, or it will look too fake).

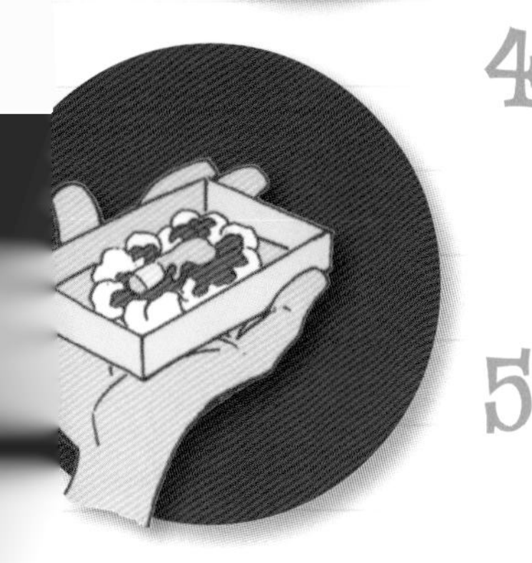

4 Put the lid on the box, and then wrap your other fingers around it so it looks like you're holding the box in the palm of your hand.

5 Go up to your victim and say, "Look what I found!" Then, open the box.

SEE WHAT HAPPENS! Your victim will be horrified looking at the cut-off finger! If your victim gets up the nerve to get up close for a better look, wiggle your finger and watch her jump!

That's a Wrap!

So, there you have it! Lots of fun stunts and pranks to thrill, scare, surprise, and gross out your nearest and dearest. Using these ideas as inspiration, why not make up some pranks of your own? And remember, stunts, practical jokes, and pranks are all about fun and laughter. So, go on out there and make people (including yourself) laugh!